The 4 Di

After

of HAPPILY EVER AFTER

Power Woman Edition

By Evangelina Hemphill

The 4 Dirty Secrets of After HAPPILY EVER AFTER (Power Woman Edition)

Copyright © 2014 by Evangelina Hemphill

ISBN: 978-0692287842

Copies of this book may be obtained at
www.evangelinahemphill.com

DEDICATION

This book is dedicated to every power woman who desires to have a World-Class Love Affair with her husband for an amazing life together for a true Happily Ever After and a career.

Here's to making the fairytale marriage you dream about become reality.

FORWARD

Evangelina has done an exceptional job unlocking wisdom in the areas of self-awareness, communication, intimacy, and sex that typically are not discussed around the kitchen or boardroom table! Her genius to bring extraordinary insight to intimate relationships allows space for couples to create the best that life has to offer. "The 4 Dirty Secrets of After HAPPILY EVER AFTER" is a phenomenal guiding light and resource tool for every relationship. It's a must-have in the currency of life.

Evangelina's ability to simplify and demystify complex relationship issues accelerates the success factor in everyone that has the pleasure to experiencing her. Evangelina has the knowledge to up level the life's of couples who want an amazing relationship with their spouse and their business. "The 4 Dirty Secrets of After HAPPILY EVER AFTER" is a must read for anyone of "power" who would like to take their relationship to the next level or who has a great relationship and is excited to see what's on the horizon.

Kelly Fidel
Speaker | Author | Sales Expert
KellyFidel.com | NoGlassCeiling.com

CONTENTS

INTRODUCTION

If you were a little girl that dreamed of having a fairytale marriage and GREW up to realize you also wanted to be a career woman, then you are reading the right book. I will share with you the four dirty secrets and how they work to create an exciting, passionate and long-term marriage.

As women, we have several things that we must balance; items, tasks, and the list goes on. The balance starts at home with our husband and children, then it takes us to our office, back home again, and everything in between. The balance of my life includes being happily married with three beautiful children and an amazing relationship with my husband who supports me… But I had to create this life.

I want women to have the option to take advantage of my successes and failures by sharing how to create "Happily Ever After." Also, I want every woman to have the option to be a sexy wife and a power house at the office. I didn't always realize this was possible. Oh but when I did, my life was forever changed.

Listening to healthy advice, I did everything they said to do—they, being my parents, my family, friends, and society: "Go to college; make good grades; get a job; have a nice life." Believe it, I did those things, and I did it well. Specific details were omitted during the advice conversations. Someone forgot to tell me if I have to hide my successes and goals from people in my life, then, those people were not the people for me; or when I get married, I have to create my own "Happily Ever After." It did not automatically happen no matter how long I waited after saying, "I do."

I instantly experienced the mommy guilt by working, growing a career, and building a business. While growing my family, I was not concerned about what other people thought or said about me. Many changes rapidly impacted my professional life. The same skills I used to be successful in the corporate environment and growing my own business were not the same skills that produced a lifelong, world-class love affair with my husband. And, last but not least, "How do I influence my husband to support my business and my career decisions?" was a question I decided to answer early in my marriage.

Once I learned how to create what I wanted in my relationship, I wanted to help other women and couples to create the type of relationship that would be best for them—no cookie cutter, no one-size-fits-all kind of marriage but true "Happily Ever After" tailor made for every couple. At a young age, I came up with the idea that there are four dirty secrets to create a "Happily Ever After". If you're like me, you grew up watching Disney movies with the prince and princess who went on amazing journeys to find love, get married, and live happily ever after.

I love Disney movies. However, all of the movies end with "I do" and a kiss. They never show you the real journey of life that the prince and the princess have to build together and how the other outside influences really impact their relationship. The movies also do not show how the lovely couple will handle those challenges and conflicts in their relationship that involve, but not limited to, different career paths, finances, children, in- laws, sex, and the list goes on.

Like any great structure of business or relationship, a solid foundation has to be built to be strong, to be lasting, and to weather any storm that may come. Self-awareness, communication, intimacy, and sex are the four secrets that are needed to have true "Happily Ever After."

Whether you're an entrepreneur or climbing the corporate ladder, these four secrets will work for you. If any one of these secrets is missing, your relationship is going to struggle and eventually, lead you down the road of unhappiness or even worse, loneliness. I'm sure you have probably been told that with having a successful career or running a seven-figure business, you can have a successful marriage, but not both.

Contrary to popular belief, you can have both a successful career and a successful marriage. This book is going to show you how. My goal is to work with women who live busy lives and are performing well in other areas of their life except in their relationship with their husbands. Some of you haven't given your relationship with your husband as much attention as you have given other areas in your life that are successful.

You don't know what you don't know, so I hope women get a true picture of what they want their relationship to be with their husbands as a direct result of reading this book. I want women to be ignited, empowered, and inspired to really believe in creating the type of relationship with their husbands that they desire.

I truly believe women should not tolerate anything less than the best life has to offer. I want women to really gain the clarity, confidence, and the charisma to create and maintain a relationship that's exciting, passionate, and long-term for true "Happily Ever After", a world-class love affair.

This book is written for women who desire to have a lifelong, world-class love affair with their husbands for an amazing life together. And ladies, husbands want this too!

Love & Happiness,

Evangelina

The 1st Dirty Secret:

Self-Awareness

Chapter 1:
What Makes You "You?"

The more you understand "you," the more your husband can understand you.

— Evangelina Hemphill

It is important to focus on you (yourself) first. It's important to focus on you as a single being first to understand your history, likes, dislikes, and perspective as to who you are. You can throw in your history as far as where you come from, who you are, who helped mold you and shape you into the person that you are today. Some other factors include previous relationships, how successful or how bad they were, how long they lasted, why they did not last, and what you liked about the person you were dating or previously married to (if you're divorced).

It's understanding who you are, that makes you "you," what makes you operate the way you operate and just understanding your perspective on life, your perspective on relationship, and how you really view yourself in terms of self-esteem, your self-confidence, and self-image.

I find that a lot of women actually understand who they truly are on the surface. In a lot of cases, I think you have some sense of who you are but know that once you understand or have a better understanding of who you are, what you like, and dislike, you are better able to communicate that to other people.

Right now, we are talking about relationships. This evolves into better communication with your husband or fiancé, who you really are and exhibiting what you really like; it is not a false pretense of just being someone for the time being. Eventually, the true "you" will come out.

Many women know who they are especially when it comes to careers and their business; but in their intimate relationships, they're struggling. Why is that? Women struggle in their relationships because there are different characteristics, different traits, and different beings (if you allow me to say) that you have to be to know where you stand.

At the office, you can be a team of one. You can just be you to do your work and to excel through the ranks. If you have your own business, if you're an entrepreneur, to really create your business and have it excel the way you want it and really succeed, there are a lot of things that you can do on your own. You can totally be a solo person and do everything at the office on your own.

Unlike being on a solo mission at the office, an intimate relationship is going to take both parties to work as a team, truthfully operate together, and function on one accord. It's not just about what you want and it's not just about your likes. It's about togetherness; what you and your spouse want; it's about what you and your spouse like and dislike or things that you don't want. It's more than just team "I"; it's the two of you coming together to create your dream team. You need skills at home that you may not necessarily have to use at the office in advancing your career.

There can be a power struggle in the relationship for women who are powerful in business because they come home and don't leave that power position at the office. I experienced this obstacle and can relate to this challenge. When you are in a position of power, whether you're climbing the corporate ladder or running a successful business, you've developed-certain skill sets to be successful. You operate in a particular way to be successful. You make sure your bases are covered and that you're always on your A-game.

Often, you may set aside being so loving, compassionate, sensitive, and empathetic; but those same skill sets that may not be on your priority list at the office are the very ones that you need in your personal relationship to be successful.

As a corporate America female engineer, those same skill sets that I used in corporate America and the skill sets that I used in my business are great but I also need additional skills to operate successfully as a wife and as a mother. Finding balance is difficult especially when you realize that you need balance. There is a different mindset and skill set that you need to be successful in both areas. You can do it but these are different skill sets. I call it my tool bag. We need different tools to complete different jobs or tasks.

I can just get the sense that a lot of women reading this book are nodding their heads in agreement with me. You completely understand. I will be giving you tools to get through this as you continue reading this book.

I ask clients, "What's your relationship with love?" and some of them say, "Well, what do you mean?" What your relationship is with love is what your vision is of love. What's your paradigm of love? What do you accept and tolerate in that area of love? Understanding what your relationship with love is will be key in understanding how you operate in your marriage and in your relationships.

If you had successful intimate relationships in the past, how successful were they if you are not with that person? Or if you've had several failed relationships in the past and you're the common denominator in those relationships, how are those affecting your marriage now? You're the common denominator to every relationship that you have. So what is your relationship with love and how was that relationship molded? Where is your paradigm coming from? What did you see your parents do? What did you see your grandparents do?

If you have older siblings, what did you observe your siblings doing? Or who painted that picture for you to start developing that sense of love? Or, where did your love come from? Who showed you love? Was it your parents or your grandparents? How about your favorite aunt or uncle? Where did that love come from? Was it your favorite kindergarten teacher? Your relationship with love will truly help you understand who you are today and where you are in your relationship.

Obviously, when it comes to "Happily Ever After," you have to look at yourself first to narrow your inner-search and look at your traits. I would say that, definitely, the single trait to look at is having an open mind and willing to try new things because it's not just you. You are in a relationship. You are married. You have to consider your spouse.

Having an open mind to discuss certain things and to try new things is all about accepting it—"I will try new things". That's half the battle, just having an open mind, be willing to try new things, and explore your new life. If you've been married for a while, explore new chapters of your life with your spouse and enjoy the journey.

My final words of wisdom here are, the more you understand "you," the more your husband can understand you because you will talk; you will act; you will walk in your true self. Your husband will respond to you as such and treat you as such. The more you understand "you," the more your husband can understand you.

Ask yourself, what is priority to you, your marriage or your career/business? Why? Be honest with yourself. If you were to say that "my priority at this point is my work but I do love my husband," what do I do? Nothing if it's not a problem. If your husband totally understands and supports your career path, then, you carry on as such. But if your husband is demanding or requesting something other than supporting your career, then, that's when the two of you need to plan a dinner date to talk about your plans for strengthening your relationship. The key is to communicate and talking about it.

Chapter 2:
Unrealistic Expectations

Don't commit to who or what you are not willing to submit to.

- Evangelina Hemphill

This could be the death of every relationship right here. But, first off, what do unrealistic expectations mean exactly? It sounds pretty simple, but I'm going to paint a picture. Expectation is a belief about, or a mental picture of the future. To be unrealistic is not being aware of expressing awareness of things as they really are. So if you have unrealistic expectations, you may not be aware of things as they really are. Your belief or mental picture of the future is off course.

A relationship needs effort, time, and care to flourish and be something great. You get out what you put in. If you're really deliberate and conscious in your decision making, you will get back more than you put in. For all couples, including my husband and I, we all have had to adapt to the other person. As wives, we have to adapt to our husbands.

But one great piece of news is that when you say, "I do," God has granted us the ability to be our husband's wife. So I have the ability to be my husband's wife any given day and be great at it. And it's the same with him. He has the ability to be my husband every day for the rest of his life and be great at it.

Unrealistic expectations may be the way you view your relationship. Unrealistic expectations could be that sense of falsehood that things are just going to happen. If you are expecting your relationship to be successful automatically, you are fooling yourself. Oftentimes, we observe other relationships maybe on television or we hear about a couple who is just "so in love", but we don't see or hear the work they invested to co-create an amazing relationship. We do not see behind the scenes what they are doing.

On the flipside, we may see this couple who appear to have an amazing relationship in public; but behind closed doors, their marriage or relationship is a wreck and an absolute mess. So you have to set your own expectations. What do you expect for your relationship so that you can work on it? Together, determine the goals of your relationship and agree on the strategy to achieve them. Have fun! You can't look at every couple that you think has a great relationship, and then try to mirror that. It will not work for you. You can't compare yourself to others. That's the death of a relationship!

It is important to have great role models who are true in the day to day delivery of their relationship. Great role modeling enables those of us who need that visual example, to reach and stretch our ability to love each other on a greater level. It is a good feeling to recognize real love.

My role models were my parents. My parents celebrated 50 years of marriage on their last wedding anniversary. And I'm the youngest of six children. My husband's role models were his God-parents, Bobby and Melba Henderson, and *The Cosby Show*. Cliff and Claire Huxtable were his couple he wanted to mirror one day once he got a family. So like their family, which was similar to my real mom and dad, everyone needs a role model to mirror.

And my mother gave me one piece of advice before I got married. She made it clear that I understood that it's not about my wedding. It's not just about that one day. That's a fun day and it is important. But the journey is the important thing and the impressive thing about a marriage is that it's lasting, successful, and happy.

If your expectations are off, I am sure you are thinking how do you change your expectations. First, except the fact that your expectations of your relationship with your husband are off. You can't be in denial about this false pretense. It allows you to hold on to that which is unreal. Holding on to the unreal is unwise.

Secondly, changing your expectations takes the desire to want a true and clear picture of your future. You want your relationship to look and be better because if it is under false pretenses and unrealistic expectations, there's no way you're happy. You can't be happy—true happiness is on the inside which includes joy about your husband and relationship. So, you must be clear that you want the best life that is available for you.

Lastly, the most important part of changing your expectations is creating a plan with your husband that will support your new, true, and clear vision of your future together. The goal is to have one plan that you both are working toward executing successfully. Your relationship can not just be on cruise control; you have to work toward your plan.

I brought up that my husband's role models were Cliff and Claire Huxtable; characters from *The Cosby Show* back in 1984. Current media has changed what's happening in relationships, with all of the reality shows. I'm a reality show fan; I do watch them. But people must understand that the "reality" shows are still scripted. It's not true reality.

Reality shows are built and scripted on drama. So no matter what show you watch, it's going to have drama to keep the ratings up. People like drama for different reason. So if you build your relationship on the drama you watch on television, you're headed down the wrong road. You're headed down the road of destruction because your marriage is not going to last. You cannot build your relationship based on a scripted drama reality show. If you do, your marriage will be a "Soap Opera".

There are probably a lot of people who watch television shows and say, "Well, that's how life is these days," and it truly isn't. Even the big screen movies often depict the materialistic side of relationships—who is buying what, the house you live in, the cars you drive. There's nothing wrong with having nice things. I like nice things. But my marriage and my relationship with my best friend, my husband, and my lover is not built on the house we live in or the cars we drive. It's built on our friendship, honesty, and loyalty to one another.

It is important to know what your relationship is built on. You, sometimes, commit to things because it sounds good or maybe you think you should; but once you head down that road, you should be committed to the decision you've made with your husband. So remember, don't commit to what you're not willing to submit to.

Chapter 3:
My Prince Charming

Prince charming is in the eyes of the beholder.
- Evangelina Hemphill

Your prince charming is whatever you want him to be. Let me start by saying the special part of the phrase, "My prince charming" or I'm going to say, your prince charming is the word "YOUR." Your prince charming should be whatever you want him to be and not what other people think he should be.

Women absolutely need to plan for their prince charming. We all plan for our prince charming one way or another. Some ladies plan with their minds and some ladies plan with their actions. The woman who plans with her mind has a plan that includes what her prince charming will act like, look like, or even his professional career, to name a few. By having these qualifications, traits, and characteristics, she prioritizes what's most important to her at that time in her life. Like any other area in your life, you need to plan what you want and desire.

You may be thinking, can I plan too much so that no man could actually live up to the expectations that I've created for my prince charming? You can! I don't think that is wise. You still have to be realistic and determine "does this person really exist?"... The one you have created in your head. I'm a firm believer in having high standards and not lowering them. The standards need to be high enough to allow you to get what you need and want but not too high that the person you're creating in your mind does not actually exist.

When I talk about making this person exist in your mind, and becoming a reality, I am not just talking about physical attraction. Identifying your prince charming for single women is not always easy. I don't mean going to look or search for men. I mean knowing what you want, what you deserve, and being clear with your expectations of a man.

Now, for a wife, it's a little bit different. She already has her prince charming. So for a wife to identify what a prince charming means to her and identify the gap between her husband and her ideal prince charming, can be challenging at times. Evaluate how much of your ideal prince charming could your husband actually be. Maybe your husband is not really meeting your expectations or he doesn't fit the mold of what you feel a prince charming should be. Ask yourself "How do I plan what my husband should be for me versus what I want in my husband?" There is a difference!

A woman has to stop thinking and talking about what she wants FROM her husband and start thinking and talking about what she wants IN her husband because there's a difference. I'll give you a financial example. A woman may want money from her husband, but she should want him to be a provider. So if all you want is money, once you get that, he has fulfilled that need for you—mission complete. But if you want your husband to be a provider, having money and being financial responsible is a given along with his commitment to take care of you. There's a huge difference between the two.

The example I mentioned was about finances. My "know what you want in your husband and not just what you want from him" philosophy should be applied to every area of your relationship. Now back to the finances. Money is not everything but we do need it to get the things we need and want. It is okay to say that you want your prince charming to be able to provide a certain level of income for your family. Absolutely, it's okay! You should definitely plan for this to be a part of your relationship goals.

Nothing is free in life. He cannot provide for you with love alone. You can't eat love and live in love. Your expenses can't be paid with hugs and kisses! However, you should not only seek out that "I want my husband to just have this crazy, enormous bank account." You're going to live a very lonely life in a big house with fancy cars. There's more to a prince charming than just finances. That's just one element. Finances and money are important but they're definitely not everything.

If your husband was your prince charming to start but, then, he's not so much anymore after some years of being together... That happens. A husband can fade out of his wife's vision of a prince charming. Life brings about changes and challenges that can easily turn your prince charming back into a frog. No relationship or marriage is above challenge or change. However, the couple that knows how to handle and survive these not so pleasurable seasons in their relationship understands the importance of routine maintenance. I have seen many times when prince charming is not so charming, when he doesn't support his wife's career or business or doesn't treat her like she's the queen of his castle.

As previously mentioned, like any other object you take care of to have it for the long haul, there's routine maintenance that has to be scheduled. This way, you make sure that "it" is operating at maximum performance. It looks how it should. It smells good. It sounds good. It is operating perfectly because of that routine maintenance. You must have that routine maintenance in your relationship so "it" operates at maximum performance.

It is possible to turn your husband into your prince charming, if he isn't already. But, again, "your" is the key word here. As a wife, you have to allow your husband to be your husband. Being a spouse is not a cookie-cutter type deal or a one-size-fits-all. Your husband is unique to you and you are unique to your husband. In order to create the type of relationship and marriage you want with your husband, you must, first, have things settled within your heart and soul in terms of your expectations.

I almost missed my prince charming. Let me tell you how. When I met my prince charming, I was a corporate engineer. I had already purchased my first home. I had a vehicle. I had travelled all over the country with my company. My prince charming was still a college student. I actually met him at a wedding and I thought—wow, this is a really great guy but, on paper, we don't add up. He's still a college student and I'm pursuing my corporate career all over the country. I like him, but it just doesn't add up. So the fact that he wasn't financially or socially where I thought he should be at the time, I almost missed out.

I had a friend who knew both of us. She said, "Okay, Evangelina, you need to wake up because your prince charming is getting ready to ride off on his white horse. You're getting ready to miss him." We all were in school at some point. Because I graduated first and started my career, he was shortly behind me. That was a wake-up call for me because she was absolutely correct. I wasn't looking at the future or potential; I was looking at the "now" at that time; and I absolutely almost missed out on one of the best things that ever happened to me.

The 2nd Dirty Secret:

Communication

Chapter 4:
Need versus Want

The better you're able to express yourself, the better you're able to communicate.

- Evangelina Hemphill

Need versus want is just a stage of understanding self and how you communicate. Good communication skills are key to succeed in life, business and relationships. Communication is only successful when both the sender (and I'll use the sender as the wife) and the receiver (the husband) understand the same information. When it is not done correctly, communication can really destroy your relationship.

The inability to communicate effectively will hold you back in your career, in society, and in your intimate relationship. So, if a woman can communicate what she needs and wants from her husband, then, he's more likely to supply or fulfill his wife's desires. As a wife, we have to take the guesswork out of the relationship so that our husbands can spend their time and energy providing what it is we actually need and want.

For example, if you want or you need to talk to your husband, you may just need to talk to him but you want him to spend quality time with you over a candlelight dinner at your favorite restaurant with your favorite songs playing in the background. But since you didn't communicate what you needed and wanted, your husband comes home 30 minutes early from the office, spends 15 of those minutes with the kids before they go to bed, and the other 15 minutes were spent checking email on his phone while talking to you.

Another example of need versus want is that you need your husband to support you in your career or your business and you want him to treat your career/business with respect and celebrate your accomplishments. But if you don't communicate this, your husband may consider your business a hobby; and he may not ever be available to care for the children so you can take business trips.

Support from your husband is a must have and is needed in every relationship; and men need support as well. If your husband understood what you needed versus what you want, he could live a happier life. He could also understand fully why this is one of the dirty secrets. So you may ask what is the want? "Want" is the extra. It's how you desire your need.

Your want is how you desire your need to look and feel. For example, a wife may say "We need to talk." But she wants to talk in a certain place, at a certain time, and in a certain atmosphere. Now, this is where a lot of couples really get off track, not understanding the need and want. Communication is huge in any relationship especially in an intimate relationship and in your marriage.

If there are breaks in the lines of communication or communication barriers, the relationship is going to suffer. There's no way to have a passionate, exciting, long-term relationship with your husband you don't or can't communicate with. When couples do not communicate, it really opens the door for all types of unwanted thoughts, beliefs, and behaviors to occur.

If your goal is to have a lifelong, world-class love affair with your husband that you can't communicate with, then, you need to schedule an appointment with me ASAP. It's not going to happen automatically. That's just not how things work!
When people are in the start of their relationship, communication is easy; but as you go along and after you say, "I do" (and that's why this book is so important), all of a sudden, the communication kind of falls apart. You can't assume your spouse is going to do a certain thing or be a certain way without talking about the relationship's needs and wants.

First, you need to know that communication isn't working or if you're communicating at all, because there's a difference. So you have to ask yourself, "Am I communicating?" Secondly, ask yourself, "How does my husband receive information?" Men process information much differently than women. And if one communication style isn't working, you have to change it because, remember, communication is successful only when both the sender and the receiver understand the same information.

If your communication is not being received by your husband, here are some steps to gain good communication skills. The first one is to know what you want to say and why. Secondly, know how you want to say it. Thirdly, listen. You have to listen. Communication is a two-way street. So after you say what you have to say, stop and listen. Finally, the two of you must reach an understanding or an agreement.

Once you have what you want to say and why you want to say it, you actually say it. You deliver the message; stop to listen for feedback from him; and then, you two reach to an understanding or agreement about what it is you're communicating about. I find that women in power have a tougher time communicating in their relationship.

As a woman in power, I found it difficult, at times, to communicate in my relationship with my husband early on. I didn't always make the best transition from office to home. I didn't always take off my corporate management hat before greeting my husband at home. And, at times, that caused our relationship to not be so exciting and passionate.

So, yes, I find that women in power have a tough time communicating their sensitive and vulnerable side in their relationship. I decided to do things differently! I had the desire to actually have a transitional phase between leaving the office and coming home. That transition phase is where I took time to actually unwind as that management person, as that corporate person to really shift gears and to become, now, wife, and when we had children, to become, now, wife and mom as I enter my home and not coming in to home as the corporate engineer.

This was a different environment, a different space, a different mindset. My husband didn't need an engineer coming home; he wanted his wife coming home. So that mental shift, that space, that transition from the office to home was huge in my success overcoming this. I think a lot of women reading this book are in the same situation. You may be the CEO or be in control at work. You come home and there's this real struggle between the business side and the tender side.

The power struggle between the business side and the tender side will occur if a woman in power is not deliberate and conscious in her decision-making as it relates to being a wife and an entrepreneur or a woman climbing the corporate ladder. There's a different skill set to be successful at both; and when mastered, a woman is irresistible to her husband and to her clients.

Being irresistible is a great place to get to. I would love to see Disney remake some of their movies: The 25th wedding anniversary of Cinderella and her prince or the 5th wedding anniversary of Princess Tiana and Prince Naveen. The remakes would be great if the focus was on the "Happily Ever After" of the relationship and the overcoming of challenges in their marriage. Even though Disney doesn't focus on that part of a relationship, "Happily Ever After" does exist once it has been created and maintained.

So the old saying, "You get out what you put in," is not exactly true in a relationship because if you don't put anything in your relationship, you will get out more than nothing. You will experience frustration and disappointment. You will get hurt and have a very unhappy, depressing relationship if you don't put anything in. However, when you put your energy, your time, and your love into your relationship, you will help create a world-class love affair. And I call that a "lifelong, world-class love affair."

One thing when I think about communication is I remember a husband sharing with me that his wife used to say that he was always on. Being an entrepreneur, he didn't let his guard down. He was always working. I had a similar situation being an engineer. As an engineer, in a predominantly male-oriented industry, I was always on. I was always on to stay on my A-game, to be the best that I could be, to perform better than my competitors and my male counterparts. So I was always on at the office and at home.

That worked great for being at the office working on projects and meeting with clients or having meetings, conferences, or workshops, but the woman that my husband married, that's who he wanted to come home. He wanted his wife to come home, his tender, loving, sexy wife—not the engineer from a corporate office who was always turned on to do an excellent job on whatever project she was working on.

The same male entrepreneur also shared that his wife would say, "I need tenderness." But he didn't understand what that meant. It was interesting because I was in the same boat as a woman. Maybe my husband didn't use those same words but that was what his message was saying to me. "I need tenderness" because I was on as an engineer all the time in that competitive, "let me be the best that I could be" industry.

So there was not a lot of tenderness. There was not a lot of compassion or sensitivity, which are the skills that you need to be successful in your intimate relationships, in your marriage. That's why I talk about it as a different skill set that you have to have to function as an entrepreneur or a career woman; and there's also a skill set you need to be successful as a wife. Once you learn to master both skill sets and how they work and complement one another, you will be freaking irresistible to your husband, your career or your clients.

What's great about this book is that women now know it's okay for you to be in this position (in work mode all the time) because you can change. You open up to more of who you really are and you can tap into your femininity without losing that competitive edge. That's really the key. When you're always "on" as a woman, sometimes, you lose a little bit of your softer side, that femininity that makes you sexy and that your husband is attracted to. You lose a little bit of it because you're always "on" in that competitive spirit.

Opening up to be more of you, being desirable to your husband, taking the time to understand who you are to him as his wife, opens up a lot of amazing doors in your relationship.

Chapter 5:
Discerning

Discerning is the ability to see and understand your husband, yourself, and your relationship clearly and intelligently.

- Evangelina Hemphill

The opposite sex can be hard to read; and, at times, when that person is the same person that shares a bed with you at night – that can be very frustrating.

First, I will start sharing about what "discerning" means. Discerning is the ability to see and understand people, things, and situations clearly and intelligently. If you can't clearly and intelligently understand your husband, see and understand things around your relationship, or understand the state in which the relationship is in, you are not reading your husband. Okay, I know that sound like a lot of pressure. But that's part of being a wife—understanding and reading your husband.

Some challenges in figuring out how to read your husband include: not seeing or understanding things that support your relationship or not having an understanding in which your relationship is in until it's too late. As entrepreneurs and business women, it's imperative that you understand your clients and your customers. You need to understand that your success lies in your ability to take information that a client provides, extract what is really being communicated, give feedback for clarity, and then create a plan that supports their needs. When you master this, you have hit the jackpot.

It works the same way with your husband. Your husband is no different. As a wife, when you understand the success of your relationship lies in your ability to process information; take information given to you by your husband, pull out what he's actually saying, and create a plan to support his needs and wants. You have yet again hit the jackpot!

You may notice how this goes back to Chapter 4. Once you get him talking and he's able to communicate with you, the real jackpot has been hit. I mean, being able to talk and communicate is really a part of intimacy. And we're going to go into intimacy a little later in other chapters.

Being able to communicate and talk is like the first step to having a successful relationship. You have to be able to communicate. That's why it's so important to me, in this book and even when working with private clients or having live events, to create and maintain success plans for couples and teach them the art of communicating with one another.

I will give some insights on how men operate. Men operate to function or behave in a particular way in everything they do. Every man is unique just as every woman is unique. Of course, it's different in every relationship. Each husband is different so that's why I am sharing so many tips in this book so you can read your husband.

It's a wife's responsibility to know her husband and not just simply understand men as a whole. My tip is you need to actually learn your husband. I learned a long time ago, even before getting married, that it's human nature to be familiar with a particular subject matter and apply that knowledge to everything you consider a part of that subject matter. And that works when you're generalizing; but it does not work when you have a unique subject matter such as your husband. He's unique to you.

I learned this, by the way, growing up. I'm the youngest of six. I did not just like being a part of "oh, you're the youngest of the six" or "oh, you're their baby sister." I wanted to be unique. Yes, I'm a part of them but I'm unique. I'm my own person. I'm more than just their younger sister. So I learned at a young age to stand out because I wanted to be my own person. So generalizing can be dangerous.

Generalizing can be very dangerous because there's nothing special about being general. I mean, generalizing is dangerous because it takes away from the important, commitment, and the ownership in a relationship. Let me give you an example. I'll use Jane. Jane is a wife versus Jane is John's wife. That's different. What makes a woman a wife is having a husband, not just any woman's husband but her own husband.

As you have to read, I've said a few times that a wife's responsibility is to learn her husband's communication style and to figure out how to read him. The word "responsibility" may offend some of you women reading this book but that is not my intent. As wives, we have certain responsibilities just as men, when they become husbands, have certain responsibilities once they say, "I do." That's the part that Disney left out. Disney didn't show that part in the fairy tale relationships and weddings.

You must learn your husband's communication style to communicate with him. You have to try this communicating thing out and test it to know how you feel about what you're saying. Wives ask yourselves; Am I comfortable with my husband and do I have confidence when I communicate with my husband? If you are hesitant about communicating with your husband and you are not sure what to say or how to say it, then, you have some homework to do. Find out the best way you can communicate and feel comfortable expressing yourself.

The ultimate communication style is to understand what makes your communication most effective, to really hit the nail on the head, and to communicate your thoughts, ideas, and feelings in a way that your husband can receive it. When I talk about communicating, I also mean you need to be aware of when you bring things to your husband.

Again, you have to know how your husband receives information. You need to know if there are certain times of the day he receives information or if there are certain tasks or activities that allow him to be relaxed enough to receive information. Just truly understanding how your husband receives information would really be a helpful communication tool for you. Of course, this teaches him how to communicate with you as well and how to read you because when you walk through the door, he knows that maybe at that point he's not going to bring up certain topics. Just understanding each other is all a part of (I'm going to use the word "responsibility" again) your responsibility to be your husband's wife and for him to be your husband.

Chapter 6:
Triple-A

The secret to love is learning the right way to love your husband.

- Evangelina Hemphill

Affirmation, acknowledge, and appreciation are the three words that can be the secret to a hot relationship. Why? These three words are powerful: affirmation, acknowledgement, and appreciation. They're going to be a mixture for a lifelong, world-class love affair.

Now, you've heard me mention "lifelong, world-class love affair." But I'm going to spend some time here to explain what that means. Let's discuss the power of each. Affirmation is the act of affirming or making a solemn declaration. So think of the power that lies within affirming how amazing, how handsome, and how smart your husband is. Affirmation really builds up a man.

Acknowledgement is to regard or describe someone or something as having or deserving a particular status. So if you make your husband know how much you need him, how he makes you so happy and you're excited that he's your husband, then, you're setting yourself up for an amazing lifelong journey with this man. Appreciation is a feeling of being grateful for something and the ability to understand the worth, quality, and importance of something. So when thinking about your life, as a whole, which includes your marriage, just think about how your husband has added to the quality of your life.

Let it not be a secret. Share your appreciation with your husband and the value that he adds to your world. And he will learn from your actions, by the way. When you start doing this, he will start doing this for you. And there's nothing that feels better in a relationship than having the Triple A: affirmation, acknowledgment, and appreciation.

I learned the Triple A, the hard way! Yes, the hard way—by doing it incorrectly and just realizing, where am I off? Okay, I'm successful at the office so, of course, or automatically, I'm going to be successful as a wife. Not so much—it's a different skill set. I am now successful at both but at the beginning, I struggled. It's important to understand the meaning of those three words, and that they're a great combination for that lifelong, world-class love affair.

My husband came alive after I used the Triple A. Men like to receive words of affirmation. That's no secret. That's any man really down to a boy. Just putting it out there, saying, and letting your husband know how awesome he is… that should be a given. He should be awesome because if you didn't pick him, you allowed him to pick you. So he should be amazing in your eyes. Remember, it's what you think, not what someone else thinks.

The importance of affirming and acknowledging the things that "your man" does for you and how he makes your world better is priceless. Everybody loves to be appreciated when they do something. But I'm talking about not just appreciating but appreciating out loud. Let him know. First, let him know. You can shout it from the rooftops and let the world know. But if he's not around, it doesn't count in his world. You have to let him know. Share these things with him.

One of the challenging part about affirming and acknowledging your man is when your relationship has faced a major challenge with infidelity, lack of trust or disappointment. It may be hard to sing his praises when you don't think that he is praiseworthy.

But, in time, of course, you can heal and it takes, as you've been reading, the communication and reading of one another to be successful. One thing you need to keep in mind, is if there's some horrible thing that's happened in your relationship and you're choosing to stay in the relationship, then, you're choosing to work on your relationship. You can't stay and then choose not to work on it because that's a suicide mission.

In most cases, when people get married, the goal is to have a "Happily Ever After" forever. To be honest, that looks different for every couple. Some may say that sounds like a fairy tale… What about the "real life story?" The real life story is having a lifelong, world-class love affair with your husband. That's the real "Happily Ever After." By using the Triple-A method you will declare, describe, and demonstrate to your husband your level of involvement and commitment to your marriage.

Expressing your love to your husband in a language he understands and likes is always a win-win for both of you. I encourage couples to take The Five Love Languages evaluation by Gary Chapman. The evaluation will allow you to understand how to love your husband and how you want to be loved. The five love languages are words of affirmation, quality time, receiving gifts, acts of service, and physical touch.
Now, I'll give you a brief overview of each one.

1) Word of affirmation: Actions don't always speak louder than words if your love language is words of affirmation. Unsolicited compliment means the world to you if this is your love language. In a lot of cases, this is men's love language, by the way.

2) Quality time: Nothing says "I love you" like full, undivided attention if your language is quality time—TV off; fork and knife down; all chores and tasks gone stand by to make sure your spouse feels truly special and loved.

3) Receiving gifts: Don't mistake this love language for being materialistic because that's not it. Receiving gifts thrives on the love and thoughtfulness and effort behind the gift.

4) Acts of service: Anytime you do something to ease the burden of responsibility that's weighing on your spouse, that's an act of service, and it speaks volumes. So the word he or she most wants to hear is "let me do that for you."

5) Physical touch: A person whose primary language is physical touch is, not surprisingly, very touchy. Hugs, pats on the back, holding hands, thoughtful touches on the arm or shoulder or face—they can all be ways to show excitement, concern, care, and love.

So those are the five love languages, in a nutshell, and they're awesome. I really believe in the five love languages. My husband and I took the evaluation at the beginning of our relationship right before we got married; and he approved so I'll share my husband's results.

My husband's love languages are words of affirmation and receiving gifts. So what I would do is buy him gifts, mostly things that he could wear, and then compliment him when he wears them. Yes, kill two birds with one stone. On the other hand, hands down, my love language is physical touch. So our running joke was "Okay, all I want is for him to be all over me and me all over him." Yes, that's what I wanted!

We had to understand how to communicate love to one another because with his love language being words of affirmation and receiving gifts, if I always wanted to do acts of service for him, that would be nice but it just wouldn't hit a spot and speak volumes to him. It would be the same with him bringing home gifts for me. It wouldn't mean as much as the touch. Don't get me wrong. I'm a lady who likes nice things. I love gifts. But my husband's kisses and hugs are priceless and no gift compares.

I was explaining to a couple that knowing your spouse love language could eliminate some issues in their relationship. It's all about speaking your spouse's language to them. I encourage every person to know their own love languages as well as their spouse's love language. Have fun speaking your husband's love language to him.

The 3rd Dirty Secret:

Intimacy

Chapter 7:
Intimacy is Not Sex

Mentally stimulating your husband has a huge Return On Investment.

- Evangelina Hemphill

When people see the word "intimacy," they automatically think that it is sex and it's not. Intimacy is one of the misunderstood words in relationships. The definition of intimacy is the state of being intimate or familiar or something of a personal or private nature.

So when couples have intimacy or are intimate with one another, they are familiar with one another. They know each other. You have to go below the surface to be intimate. You need to dig deep to be familiar with your husband. On the surface is the basic information such as where they went to high school, where they went to college, or where they currently work and maybe knowing what foods they may be allergic to or even knowing the type of relationship they have with their parents. Surface level information is information you would find out in a general conversation with the person.

So all that information may also be known by someone you're standing next to in the store or someone you catch a cab with. It's not personal information, so there's nothing private about it. However, going deeper is going to require some time and effort to truly be intimate and familiar with your spouse.

Intimacy is a much deeper level than just the surface of knowing someone or thinking that you know someone. Oftentimes, this is what's special about a marriage because the "raw" you comes out when being intimate. The raw you or the naked you (not literally naked) has to be exposed so your spouse can really know who you are by you opening up.

It means something different for men and women; and it looks different as well. To be intimate is sharing your dreams, your goals—to let your spouse into your private space. A man's intimacy level is not as high as a woman's and I say that not to compare the levels but for the understanding of it. Men get to know their women at the beginning of their relationship like when they're dating; as time goes on—you get married, you have a career, you're growing a business, you may even have children so the make-up of who you are as a woman changes.

But, in some cases, the men hold on to what they first learned about their wives in the beginning when they were dating; and he really doesn't update his internal database with what's up to date with her and with current information. "The Husband" tries to continue the relationship with his wife with the information he had when he first met her, and not understand that she's changed; or he notices the change but he doesn't take the time to get up to date and be current with who she is today.

For a woman, intimacy is part of who she is. A woman is more in tune with her inner being, which allows her to connect better with her husband. Most women have a high level of attention to detail for people and things that they care about. Women are more willing to open up and share their inner thoughts and feelings and more willing to adapt to her husband's habits.

Hopefully, you can help your spouse and yourself be more intimate after reading this chapter. But, first, I need to really break down here that it's not about sex; yet, society always thinks it is. So if you go to your spouse and say, "I want to talk about intimacy," they're automatically going to think that it's a discussion about sex.

Everywhere you look, there's sex—television, radio, etc. Society has taken the easy road using sex to promote things. The physical act of sex is not hard to do. Some couples are missing an important piece of their relationship. Having intimacy in your relationship takes time and effort with the benefits being well worth the time and energy.

Intimacy looks like being in sync or becoming one with your husband. A man being intimate looks like him showing his insecurities and then knowing that his wife will support him in whatever he has to say. A woman being intimate looks like her exposing her true feelings about herself to allow her husband to know her better. Sometimes, being intimate also looks like being inconvenienced at times. Let me share with you a personal example.

My husband, Jason, is a huge football guru. I mean, he played and coached on both the collegiate and professional level. So when we met, the only thing I knew about football was the outfit I would wear if I were going to attend a game. That was pretty much it. But since football was such a huge part of his life, I took the time and put in the effort to learn the game. So, now, we talk football. We watch football. We attend games together, which really allowed me to enter deeper into his world.

We have some phenomenal conversations. We have made some lifelong memories and have participated in some amazing lovemaking all in the name of football because I made the decision to dig deeper, understand, and learn about a huge part of his world. So it wasn't about football at all. It was about understanding and connecting with my husband on a higher level to develop that mental stimulation.

I learned football because I care about my husband. He got that feeling that I care and he knew that I was taking steps to be closer to him by learning all about football; and he appreciates that; and we're able to reciprocate an appreciation of each other because of that steps that I took. So it wasn't actually about football, it was about understanding and knowing my husband. Now, I love football!

There are many ways to become more intimate. First, it's going to require you to have the desire to understand and connect with your husband on a higher level. And I'll give you three tips to become more intimate.

The first tip is spending quality time together talking. Just talking... it doesn't have to be any particular topic but just putting out there how you feel about certain things and how your day was or just what's on your mind. The second tip is showing your spouse affection—holding hands. It could be hugging; it could be kissing; it could be a pat on the butt when you walk by just showing affection of some sort. The third tip is participating in an activity with one another other than sex, participating in an activity where it takes both of you working together to accomplish one goal.

I hope you see how important intimacy is in a relationship. If you have ever been hurt on an intimate level, you may be asking yourself, is there a way you can rebuild the intimacy in your relationship? Yes, you can. Intimacy can be rebuilt. It will take time and you need to be deliberate in your decision-making. The four tips to use to become more intimate will also work with rebuilding intimacy.

The first tip is spending more time together talking about how you want to rebuild your relationship. It shouldn't be a secret. You have something that occurred in your relationship and trying to avoid it is not going to make it go away. So spend that time to just talk and to connect; and, sometimes, share how you want the relationship to work and how you're going to rebuild it.

The second tip is to show your spouse affection when operating in their love gift. It's doing the five love language evaluation and then you showing your spouse love with their love language. You don't speak your language to them; you speak their language to them. The third tip is to participate in an activity with one another that requires you to trust your spouse. You have to trust them to do their part to complete the mission.

Last but not least, the fourth tip is to pray together. Prayer is a very private and intimate moment. If you're able to pray with your spouse and be thankful for what you've been blessed with. You should pray for what you are anticipating to take place in your live as well. Pray about what you want to happen in your life, if you can pray with your spouse and share that moment and connection, that's a huge way of being intimate without saying, "Hey, let's sit down and be intimate." As you're praying, you are actually sharing what your inner thoughts are. You're sharing that personal space with your spouse when you pray together.

As I wrap up this chapter, I want to explain the great connection between intimacy and sex. Intimacy is not sex although they work great together. I talked about intimacy as being intimate or familiar with your spouse to allow them into your personal or private space. Sex is a physical act of allowing a person into your personal space that often includes sexual intercourse.

So let me paint the picture for you, ladies. Just imagine having a husband who mentally stimulates you. He says the things that you need to hear. He lets you know how he can't resist you. As he kisses you and allow his hands to explore your body, his body confirms that he wants to make love to you… Now, I'll let you finish the story and put your end on it. But this is an example of how intimacy and sex work well together. Think about having that sexual experience with your husband who also mentally stimulates you. That is going to be some mind-blowing sex!

.

Chapter 8:
Be Vulnerable

Letting your husband know you will eliminate him trying to figure you out.

- Evangelina Hemphill

Being vulnerable is a huge part of a relationship. It's bigger than you and your husband sharing a house, having children together, or even sharing finances. Being vulnerable is a solo mission. It is all you. It involves you exposing your most personal and private thoughts and desires; and that's not always easy.

It can be difficult because you're really taking the blinders off and exposing who you really are, what you think about, your desires, your passions, and your fears. It's really putting you on a table to let everyone into your world. But what's sad about this is that so many people have been hurt so they do not want to be vulnerable. Hurt can make you close yourself off from the world and shut down. Hurt will make you create your own world for just yourself even though you are operating with everyone else at home, in your business, or just in society as a whole.

Being vulnerable is key to achieving "Happily Ever After" and a real lifelong, world-class love affair. It is because you're laying it all on the line. You're making your expectations, desires, dreams, and fears known. Once you have made them known, your husband is more likely to fulfill his role in those areas. I shared in a previous chapter that in putting everything on the table, you can take the guess work out of the equation for your husband. The whole goal is to allow him the opportunity to be the husband to the true "you."

It can be scary. Been there, done that, and it was not easy. Women of power whether entrepreneurs or executives, we learn to mask and not show our vulnerability; and, notice, I said "we." I'm included in that number. The scary thing about being vulnerable is that you have no control over how your husband handles the information or what he'll do with the information. But his love, commitment, and loyalty should allow him to handle and treat your vulnerability with respect and dignity, with no judgment.

I have four tips for the person who is having a hard time opening up. The first tip is to know what you want to share with your husband and why. The second tip is to understand how your husband processes information so you will know how and when to share with him. The third tip is to be prepared to get feedback as your husband is processing to gain understanding. The fourth tip is to have high hopes that the shared information will bring you and your husband closer together.

Now, what about opening up to your husband? Will he just open up because you opened up? Unfortunately, men don't work that way. When getting your husband to open up, remember these tips, ladies. First, start small. Encourage whatever information he wants to share with you without requiring more. So don't be pushy to get more. No matter how small the information or how big a piece of information he wants to share, receive it. Secondly, use active listening skills. Don't interrupt. Allow him to express himself, how he needs to, for however long with just listening, with no feedback at that point. Thirdly, don't judge. Accept the thoughts he shared without judging him. Judging will make your husband shut down and put his information back in his vault. Close the door and throw away the key—so no judgment. Ask any man and he will give me the thumbs up here. He will totally agree with me.

With all the technology we have access to these days, it can be difficult for couples to walk away from the distractions that go on all around them and truly open up. Distractions that we have readily available include smart phones, iPads, and even a laptop. There's nothing intimate about sharing your inner thoughts while your spouse is chiming in every few seconds with, "Uh-huh, Okay, Uh, Yeah" because they're checking email on their phone while you're sharing.

Even though people are capable of multitasking by listening to their spouse and checking email, it tells the person who's talking that what they're sharing is not important enough for you to give them your undivided attention. It appears that you don't care. I share this because couples continue to not give their undivided attention while trying to have a deep, intimate conversation with their spouse.

They do it because they're mindset is, "I can multitask. I can check these emails. I can send this text. I can read this document and listen and respond." Yes, you can but you're sending the wrong message to the person who's sharing. You are not very emotionally connected when this happens. Sometimes, women open up to their husbands when he is not in the mode to "receive." Knowing when to open up is just as important as knowing how your husband processes information.

I hope everything you're reading is making perfect sense to you. Sharing at the wrong time can be very difficult when your husband is not receiving the information. Notice, I mentioned the receiving and the transmitting of communicating. They both work together. It's in knowing when the best time to share and then understanding how he processes information so you're sharing at the right time and the right way for a great outcome.

Women should be aware of using their great communication skills before opening up because, again, you want to communicate the right message. You want to be clear in your message and clear in the delivery of how you feel and what your thoughts are. If you're sharing desires or fears, you want to make sure you use great communication skills to clearly display and paint the picture to your husband as to what you need to say.

Chapter 9:
Outside the Bedroom

Having your spouse as your best friend will turn you on outside and inside the bedroom.

- Evangelina Hemphill

Outside the bedroom is just as important as inside the bedroom because they are both a part of intimacy. Knowing what turns you on outside of the bedroom is going to take a little more effort than just having sex. It's really digging deep and understanding who your spouse is. Since you've been following along in the previous chapters Intimacy Is Not Sex and Being Vulnerable, I know those have been very powerful. In fact, I hope you've learned a tremendous amount reading those chapters.

I understand how deep outside the bedroom can really go and how this is the secret to having that world-class love affair, you want. When you have your world-class love affair, it feels like "mission complete." It's all about understanding what outside the bedroom means to you, how you can apply it, and how it relates to your relationship.

Along with men, several women even think intimacy is sex. So it's not shame-on-you for not knowing. It's just understanding the differences between intimacy and sex; just understanding and comprehending what the differences are and then how well they work together. It's digging deeper than what is inside the bedroom because once you go outside the bedroom and connect, it's going to make inside the bedroom that much more exciting.

In my marriage, one thing that worked in our favor at the beginning of our relationship was that we were best friends before we became a dating couple. Then, we were engaged and got married. The fact that we've built our relationship on a strong foundation of being friends has truly been the difference in being successful in our marriage. There's probably a ton of you women reading who are saying, "I wish my husband was my best friend."

Your spouse should be your best friend. It's very possible for him to be your best friend. Let's talk about the qualifications of a best friend. A best friend is a person whom you can trust and enjoy spending time with. You can count on them to be loyal and faithful to the relationship that you both share. A best friend is someone you look forward to seeing. You plan ways to spend time together. It's someone you support and stand behind 100%.

A best friend also knows your life story inside and out because you trust them enough to expose your true self to them. All the qualifications and requirements of a best friend are also the qualifications and requirements of a great spouse. My husband and I became best friends before we started dating. When we met, we made a decision that we really did want to like each other and then love each other. So we became best friends and started dating. We started our lifelong, world-class love affair early on. The two of us being best friends has truly helped our relationship be happily ever after.

A friendship is what makes a relationship fun. It makes it exciting. I wouldn't trade anything for my husband being my best friend. Sure, I have close female friends and we spend time together, we share and we talk. But my best friend is my husband. I know that's why my husband and I are able to talk so freely about what "turns" us on.

Knowing what turns you and your spouse on outside the bedroom is a huge part of intimacy in your relationship. And this is not a guessing game. You have to know and apply these secrets and tips that I've shared in this chapter so far to get this part right. Knowing what turns you on outside the bedroom is a combination of self-awareness, communication, and intimacy in your relationship long before you even get to the sex. And it's equally important to you for your husband to know what turns you on outside of the bedroom.

What turns you on outside the bedroom is something that your husband should have taken the initiative to find out over the course of your relationship. And taking the initiative to know what turns you on outside of the bedroom definitely increases your husband's success rate inside the bedroom. I know women from all over the world agree 100% with me!

In the event your husband doesn't remember or just needs a refresher, you have to take the initiative to communicate what turns you on outside the bedroom. Try to leave clues to allow him to figure it out with your guidance. If your husband doesn't have a clue, then, you're going to need to hold his hand and walk him through the process as you show him and teach him "you."

I shared in an earlier chapter that intimacy is a state of being familiar, intimate or something of a personal and private nature. So when couples have intimacy in their relationship and are intimate with one another, they are familiar with each other. They know each other. There is no way you and your husband have a high level of intimacy in your relationship and you two are not familiar with one another. A high level of intimacy is not going to happen if you are not familiar with each other. Remember, being intimate is about knowing your spouse.

If you are asking yourself, how do you bring up having a higher level of intimacy to your husband? Do just that... Bring it up. If you and your husband don't have a high level of intimacy, you both already known that even though it's not being discussed. You know if your husband knows you by his actions and by the things he says to you. Intimacy is a critically important area of a relationship but a not talked about subject.

The 4th Dirty Secret:

Sex

Chapter 10:
Taking Charge in the Bedroom

Taking charge in the bedroom is a power move.
- Evangelina Hemphill

Ladies, taking charge in the bedroom is a dirty little secret because it allows you to have a voice in the bedroom and lead. This isn't just common knowledge. Nothing is common sense. You don't know what you don't know. The lady taking charge in the bedroom doesn't lead into a power struggle. A woman taking charge in the bedroom is a power move for her; and her man is going to love it. But there are some misconceptions when it comes to sex. Here are some misconceptions about sex: one, men have a secret handbook about sex; second, men always know what to do to pleasure women; third, men should always take charge in the bedroom. All of those are misconceptions. None of them are completely true.

The misconceptions are a little bit of Hollywood because this is what we're seeing on television and in movies. It doesn't take the power away from your man when you take the lead in the bedroom. A woman having a voice and leading in certain situations in the relationship doesn't lessen the power of her man. It gives your husband a chance to sit back and really enjoy what's going on.

Let's break down a few of these "taking charge in the bedroom" challenges. Your husband, above all things, is looking forward to the end result, which is the climax. In the process of reaching their climax, men want their wives to be open to try new things. New things may be different sexual positions, making love outside of the bedroom, and even playing with toys. It's all about having an open mind as you reach the end result.

A wife expects to be treated like she is the sexiest, most beautiful woman in the world and her husband can't resist her. She expects her husband to make it known that he belongs to her and she's the only woman for him. When husbands make this information public, they are working toward an amazing relationship with their wife.

Wives are extremely important. It is important not to just let your husband take charge and only do what he wants to do in the bedroom. Making love involves both of you. It takes both the wife and the husband to create an exciting, passion-filled, romantic love affair with one another.

Sometimes, he will lead; and, sometimes, she will lead. With each and every lovemaking experience, the couple needs to be mentally and physically present to have an amazing time together. I am covering this for the women that may not feel comfortable leading. And for others, where their husband may not be comfortable giving up that lead or that role of being in charge to allow his woman to lead and be in charge.

But when it comes to this book, I'm focusing on women who are power women. A woman in power, whether she's in corporate America or she's a successful entrepreneur that is used to being the lead. She's used to making those power decisions, so to come home as second in command... What does that look like? What does that feel like?

It's about understanding her role and letting go in certain situations. Been there, done that, so I'm speaking from personal experience. Let your husband do what he needs to do as the man in your life. With women taking charge in the bedroom, it allows their husbands to sit back and enjoy the experience from a different point of view and perspective.

This is important for sexual health. Like any great relationship, it takes two. So a couple's sexual health is the overall condition of their bodies and minds involving sex. Having great sexual health is a must for any marriage.

At this point, you've gone through the self-awareness and you know who you are. You know rules of communication so you understand the best way to communicate your needs and wants from the second dirty secret. Then, you took a deep dive into intimacy learning how to connect on a deeper level. Sex is just the icing on the cake. When you have all those other three secrets in place, the sex is going to be awesome; it's going to be amazing.

So I am standing up saying, "Listen, ladies, we need to communicate what we like and what we don't like." Women need to communicate what they like and don't like to their husbands. This should not be a secret.

It doesn't do a woman any good to keep her sexual desires to herself. Ladies, your husbands should know and have your sexual desires and pleasures locked into his memory bank. It should not be a secret and he should not be forced to try to figure out what's right and what's wrong concerning you on his own.

Men are not mind readers. Women need to be open and honest about what satisfies them in the bedroom. It has been known, for women, to fake their satisfaction or climax instead of taking the time to talk to their husbands about what they expect and want during their lovemaking. That's not good because it may seem like, "oh, I'll just fake it so it's innocent," but it's not innocent. It's being deceptive. Faking is not being true to your husband in letting him know what was really going on and how you are not being satisfied.

I want you to think about the importance of taking charge in the bedroom. Women taking charge in the bedroom and leading, she's going to enjoy herself and her husband will sing her praises. The saying, "A man wants a lady in the street and a freak in the bedroom," still stands true today. That has not ever changed and it won't ever change.

Chapter 11:
Oral + Intercourse = An Orgasm

Oral sex and intercourse is a great combination to create an orgasm.

- Evangelina Hemphill

This is all about oral sex and intercourse working together to create an awesome orgasm. Unfortunately, there are a lot of women who are very uncomfortable with oral sex. There are many different reasons why women are uncomfortable with oral sex. Some of the reasons include male hygiene, their own hygiene, bodily fluids, and moral views. These reasons have made oral sex not as desirable as intercourse.

Some women say oral sex adds to their sexual relationship in a negative way. These negative views has taken the beautiful, sexy, passionate sensual experience between a husband and a wife and made it degrading or shameful for some women. Sex was created by God for a husband and wife to pleasure and satisfy one another. Sex should be a private sacred experience between a wife and her husband.

But, sadly, even just talking about oral sex or intercourse is going to have some women very uncomfortable. There are many married couples who are uncomfortable talking about oral sex, intercourse, or even anal sex. I don't mean taking part or performing any of it. I mean merely talking about it. So I ask couples, "How do you feel comfortable taking part in it and performing oral sex or having intercourse if you can't even talk about it?"

A wife should not have to be uncomfortable or feel ashamed to talk about something that she has signed up to do when she said, "I do." Sex is part of the deal when you signed the dotted line. Discussing oral sex or intercourse should be a very comfortable and natural conversation between a husband and wife. It has to be in that safe place—communication—which I covered in the second secret where couples have a sex conversation.

Now, if a woman has barriers and needs help breaking through the barriers to have a great sex life, then keep reading. A woman can break through barriers to have a great sex life by understanding her own personal relationship with sex, understanding how she feel about sex and knowing why she feel this way.

Sharing this information with your husband will be very powerful. There are many different factors that go into a woman's current relationship with sex. Understanding your history with sex will allow you to overcome and break through barriers to have a great sex life with your husband. For example, oral sex provides the clitoral stimulation needed for a woman to have an orgasm. Fifty to seventy-five percent of women who have orgasms need the clitoral stimulation or they're unable to have an orgasm through intercourse alone. This is information every woman and man should know.

So it's okay if you're in this situation because there are a lot of women who find sex unfulfilling because they don't have an orgasm as easily as they may see in the movies. Those movies will have you messed up in your relationship and do not demonstrate a real life situation. Those movies are scripted so there isn't much time and room for reality to take place.

The actors in movies are trained and they get paid to create this mood at any given time on any given set with anybody. There's nothing intimate about that. A woman has to know and understand her body, which allows her to be able to have an orgasm. Knowing how and when you need to be touched or penetrated along with if and when you want oral sex will create that real orgasm that you're looking for.

I have also noticed how the Christian community has a very tough time with openly talking about sex. As a Christian, I can truly shed some light on this subject. As I've shared earlier, God created sex for a husband and wife to pleasure one another but the world has made it okay to do and have sex with anybody, anywhere. With the world making sex their own, it's as if the Christian community has made the open discussion of sex off limits and ungodly to do.

Married couples which include Christian couples are the very ones that should be having an amazing mind-blowing sex life. But there's no way they're doing that with their spouse if they can't talk about it. Sex is boring to some Christian couples. These couples are not communicating in the way they should be, and the husband and wife have their fears and insecurities.

When I started my business years ago, I saw the need to help Christians with this much-needed area, but no one wanted to talk about it. The subject was, and still is, sex! I actually started a program for Christian wives, and I went into great detail about the areas of self-awareness, communication, intimacy, and sex in the marriage—the four dirty secrets that we're talking about today.

The wives who took and finished the program left confident. They were able to communicate the type of relationship they wanted with their husbands. They gained the charisma to really have an intimate relationship with their husbands and maintain a relationship that is exciting, passionate, and long term for true "Happily Ever After" or a lifelong, world-class love affair. The transformations were amazing!

It's too bad that more couples don't talk about their sex life. They just kind of go through life thinking, well, this is how it's going to be because "my wife doesn't like this" or "my husband doesn't understand that." There should be a conversation so the thinking can change to "Hey, let's give it a try." Some of those barriers that I've talked about earlier are the mental barriers, just your perception of performing the act or having the act of oral sex performed on you due to past situations. You can't fault your current husband for things that went wrong in previous relationships. That's not fair to your husband.

In a relationship, you must be open in the bedroom and willing to communicate. So for all you "orgasm fakers"... Stop faking. Faking an orgasm is bad, bad, and bad because a woman is not actually being satisfied and she's leading her husband to believe that she is. Being anxious or worried or feeling pressure to have an orgasm with your husband can work against you, ladies. Anxiety can create tension and an orgasm is a relaxed experience. Tension and orgasms are not compatible and don't work well together.

If you're wondering—"Am I doing it right?"; "Is he judging me?"; "Am I having fun?"; "Does he like this?"—Those things will create a very anxious atmosphere. An orgasm is not going to happen. So give yourself permission to let go, relax, and have that internal dialogue saying, "You know what, I'm a part of this exchange. I do have the right to ask for what I want. I do have the right to say how I'm feeling." You don't have to have such high expectations for yourself. Just give yourself permission to relax and go with the flow.

Chapter 12:
Sexual Creativity

Look forward to exploring one another's bodies and try new sex positions with your husband.
                                    - Evangelina Hemphill

Creativity, of course, can be the cure for boredom. A boring sex life will initially dry up the sex, and there won't be any sexual activity at all. Sex is just as important to a marriage as self-awareness, communication, and intimacy. Having a creative sex life is a part of your story in having that lifelong, world-class love affair.

Sex is a deep connection that you have with just one other person on the planet. That's correct—one other person, your spouse, not many people. I mean, having a sexual experience with your husband and making love is so special and so needed for our health and well-being. It's a part of what we do as being married. In the last chapter, I really talked about some of the things that made people uncomfortable. But if you break through this, creativity is another way to connect in your relationship.

Suggestions for being creative are endless so I'll cover just a few. Let's talk about the G-spot. The G-spot is described as an erotic zone located in the inner walls of the vagina along the course of the urethra that will swell during sexual stimulation. Now, there have been myths. Is the G-spot really real? Yes, it's really real. Whether or not it's going to do for you what you've heard it can do is another story.

You may not find that myth is what you're looking for. So I'm going to give you some different suggestions on creativity that you can explore and have fun with. I'm going to give you six to boost your creativity today.

1) Do it yourself. This means show your husband what you would like done to you. Use his hands and you move them. Create and paint the picture. Show him the path of what you actually want.

2) Talk to your husband. Verbal communication is the easiest way to let your husband know that you like what he's doing; "It" excites and pleasures you.

3) Let your fingers, hands, elbows do the talking. Use all your body parts. Get your whole body involved. Leave nothing on the table. Leave no area unexplored.

4) Mix it up in the middle. There's no certain order. Whether you do foreplay, have oral sex, or intercourse, whatever it is that you do, there's no certain order to make it happen and create the magic for you and your husband.

5) Cum first and cum later. This takes off the pressure of having "The Orgasm" as if it's only going to be one. Take the pressure off and have

in mind that you can and it's okay to have more than one orgasm in the same sexual experience.

6) Experiment with sexual positions. Mix it up. Change it up. Don't do the same position that you always do every time.

These six tips will help with starting to create and boost that creativity in your sex life.

I promote trying different sex positions to keep things exciting. I'm going to share with you five tips to consider when selecting sex positions.

1) Find the right physical position. You and your husband are probably different sizes at different heights with different flexibility levels. So find the right position that's going to give you what you're looking for.

2) Move different during different positions. You could do the same position but if you move differently, it's going to give you a different result.

3) Adjust the angle of penetration. You may have this one position that you really like but to change things up and to make it a little different, you can change the angle of penetration, which is going to give you a different feel.

4) Get the rhythm. Finding the rhythm to whatever sex position you're in is going to help with the connection and the harmony of you and husband.

5) Locate the speed and pace. Your speed and pace in a position will allow a different feel, a different penetration along with the angles; and it's going to give you or let you know if this is or is not the sex position for you.

There are many sex positions, as many as there are names for them. One of the most common sex position tried is the missionary sex position with the woman on her back and the man on top. Everyone who has ever had sex has tried this position. One of the most commonly talked about sex positions is the doggie style sex position. In this position, your husband is penetrating you from behind. This position can be done on your knees, your hands, standing on your feet, or even bending over a bed or a chair. When done right, this position is a win-win for both parties.

Woman on top position is another common position that has you sitting on top of your husband facing him with your knees bent and shins on the ground. A way to spice this up is to bring your knees up and place your feet on the ground. It's better known as the "cowgirl" sex position. The reverse cowgirl position is also a spinoff of the woman on top with you facing away from your husband. This position gives you the benefit of having complete control of thrust, angle, and movement.

And the list goes on. I mean, I could name a list of different positions but the whole point is trying different things to spice it up and not do the same old position every time in the same place. You may do the same position but if you do it in a different place and atmosphere, it's going to give you a different spin and feel.

I've work with a lot of couples and I've had to explain this to them... Oftentimes, women come to me because they think they have a sex problem. And sex is just the end result. Their bigger problem is one of the other three secrets. I hear "Hey, we have a sex issue. We have a sex problem." My reply is "Okay, tell me what the issue is."

As women share with me, I discover that it's actually not the sex at all. Both bodies are more than capable of having sex, but there are issues beneath the surface that affect their sex life. When I help create a plan to improve the marriage, the magic can happen... Great loving making that is!

CONCLUSION

Creating a true Happily Ever After is a process. If you knew some of what was shared in this book prior to reading it, learned more about a topic, or have been exposed to totally new information, it all is going to allow you to see a bigger picture and a different variation of your marriage to make your relationship the way you've always wanted it to be.

I have given some great information on how to become aware of what it is that you truly want. Then, I've given tools to make sure that you're communicating properly; and, of course, that can be difficult but you can work through it, right? I know the benefits of great communication from personal experience and watching the transformation in other couples relationship. The very secrets, tips, and best practices in this book are the very ones that transformed my marriage along with many others.

You can always read this book again and again because I started working with self-awareness and moved right into communication. Then, I went to the deeper place of intimacy which leads us to have fun and be creative with sex. Passionate-exciting sex is a reward for both the husband and wife.

I know that when I teach this and talk about the four dirty secrets, sex is the secret men remember. I was in a VIP Day once and there was a couple there and we talked about the 4 dirty secrets. We took a break and when we came back, the only secret that the husband remembered was sex. His memory was amusing to everyone because great sex is the prize in a marriage. But before you get the prize, you have to know the other secrets that lead to the prize.

Having a spouse to share your life with is a privilege. Don't take your husband for granted nor should he take you for granted. Create the life you both want by exploring life together. Be best friends. Enjoy one another. Communicate and be able to talk about anything, anytime, anywhere. Love your husband and stay in love with him.

Writing this book has also been a journey. I thank you for being a part of this journey. I'm so glad you've read this book, The 4 Dirty Secrets of After HAPPILY EVER AFTER. I am confident anybody who reads this book and applies what I have shared is going to have an amazing marriage. I pray that it has blessed you tremendously. I would love to hear your personal story of how your marriage has been transformed from where you were to your Happily Ever After. Your story could be featured on my website. You can contact me at:

evangelina@evangelinahemphill.com

www.evangelinahemphill.com

Here's to your HAPPILY EVER AFTER and living an amazing life with your husband!

THE NEXT STEPS TO YOUR HAPPILY EVER AFTER

Today is your day! It is the day you can make a change. Stop the struggle to find that one thing that's going to make your relationship with your husband perfect and understand it is a process. You have the desire to have a wonderful marriage, yet your relationship is still not full of the great communication, excitement, and passion needed to create a Lifelong World Class Love Affair! I have several tools that will give you the information you need to have a true Happily Ever After. Simple log on to my website at **www.evangelinahemphill.com** to take advantage of these great tools:

- ✓ Sign-up on my home page for my FREE bi-weekly email newsletter featuring amazing tips and information on how to create the relationship you desire and how to keep it.

- ✓ To make a significant shift in your marriage and personal life, I invite you to click on the "Work With Me" tab on my website to learn about working with me privately.

- ✓ If you are looking for a speaker for your next event, from a church social to a corporate boardroom, that delivers fresh powerful content, I am here for you. You can connect with me on my "Contact Us" tab on my website. Fill out the needed information and click SEND.

Author's Quotes

Chapter 1: The more you understand you, the more your husband can understand you.

Chapter 2: Don't commit to who or what you are not willing to submit to.

Chapter 3: Prince charming is in the eyes of the beholder.

Chapter 4: The better you're able to express yourself, the better you're able to communicate.

Chapter 5: Discerning is the ability to see and understand your husband, yourself, and your relationship clearly and intelligently.

Chapter 6: The secret to love is learning the right way to love your husband.

Chapter 7: Mentally stimulating your husband has a huge Return On Investment.

Chapter 8: Letting your husband know you will eliminate him trying to figure you out.

Chapter 9: Having your spouse as your best friend will turn you on outside and inside the bedroom.

Chapter 10: Taking charge in the bedroom is a power move.

Chapter 11: Oral sex and intercourse is a great combination to create an orgasm.

Chapter 12: Look forward to exploring one another's bodies and try new sex positions with your husband.

ACKNOWLEDGMENTS

It was a wintry season in my marriage and disappointments in my professional career that changed the course of my life. After seeking God and standing on his promises, I decided to create a real Happily Ever After with my husband and help other women do the same with their husband. I thank God for the opportunity to help couples have the God-kind-of-marriage. God gets the glory.

To my mother, Diannia M. Hammond: Thank you for loving me unconditionally! Thank you for being a woman of integrity, wisdom, guidance, and always showing your support in my endeavors. I thank God for allowing me to be your daughter.

To my daddy, the late great William Howard Hammond, Sr: Thank you for always allowing me to be me. I will always be your "working girl." I love and miss you dearly!

To my siblings, Tammy (Guy), William (Jeanna), Jerisia, Daniel, and Claymond (Angela): Thank you all for the life lessons. It has been a blessing to be the youngest of you all, be able to learn from you, and grow to thrive as the person I am today. I love you all!

To my nephews and nieces (my first babies) Eustachio, William, Shanesha, Kionna, Deontay, Jeremy, Areale, Diannia, Isreal, Guy, Jira, and Zereal: In helping raise you, you helped raise me. Thank you for allowing me to be your aunt.

To my spiritual parents, Drs. Herbert and Marcia Bailey, thank you for helping create spiritual stability in my life and teaching me the principles of enduring "the process" of overcoming challenges to succeed.

To my first set of clients (my cousins), Johnny-Mae, Stesha, BJ, Rena, Jerri, Shelby, Akeva, Jessica, Brittany, Daniella, Tre', Phillip, Patrick, and Strawell: Thank you for allowing me to start my relationship consulting firm as a child by consulting with all of you on your relationships during family gathers.

To my friends Tonya and Lakeesha: Your friendship and sisterhood means so much to me. You two have touched my life in so many ways and I love you for it.

To my proofers, Germaine Smith, Jerisia Barnes, and Jerri Smith: Thank you for taking the time to proof my drafts. Your feedback and words of wisdom are priceless.

To my three beautiful children, Jason II, Jordan, and Joey: Thank you for loving me and always supporting my work. I thank God for the opportunity to mold and shape you. I consider it a privilege and honor to be your mother.

To my Big Daddy, best friend, husband, lover, and real-life Prince Charming, Jason Matthu Hemphill: You have believed in me and supported me from the very first day we met. For that I am eternally grateful. You being a part of my life have made my world amazing. Thank you for always being my number one fan. I love you so much and look forward to continuing our life journey together!

ABOUT THE AUTHOR

Evangelina Hemphill, industrial engineer turned relationship consultant, is a sought-after speaker, author, and marriage expert whose passion is to help couples stop just being married in favor of having a Lifelong World Class Love Affair with their spouse for an amazing life together. She is a graduate of South Carolina State University and holds a Bachelors of Science in Industrial Engineering Technology. After graduation, Evangelina started her professional engineering career with United Parcel Service. Evangelina is currently the owner of The Hemphill Agency and founder of Hemphill Publishing.

Evangelina truly believes in "Happily Ever After" after saying the words "I do." She grew up the youngest of six children while learning from her parents how a marriage should work and the importance of family. Evangelina watched her father travel the country, provide financially, and allowed Evangelina the freedom to be herself. She also watched and learned from her mother up close as her mother ran the day to day household business. Evangelina learned the foundation of being a person of integrity, business women, wife, and mother from her amazing parents. Evangelina was privileged to help her parents celebrate 50 years of marriage on December 15, 2013!

Learning from family and using her education along with her God given ability, Evangelina desires to help women create the type of marriage that is long-lasting. No cookie cutter or one size fit all type of marriage but true Happily Ever After for every couple tailor made. Evangelina believes people should not tolerate anything less than the best life has to offer. Through her seminars and speeches she conveys the message to gain the clarity, confidence, and the charisma to create and maintain a relationship that's exciting, passionate, and long-term for true "Happily Ever After"... World-Class Love Affair. Evangelina resides in Columbia, South Carolina, with her amazing husband, Jason, and their 3 beautiful children, Jason II, Jordan, and Joey.

WORKS CONSULTED

1. Sensual Pathways to Pleasure, Robert W. Birch, Ph.D., PEC Publishing 2006

2. U.S. National Library of Medicine: www.nlm.nih.gov

3. Dictionary Online: www.merriam-webster.com

4. The 5 Love Languages, Gary Chapman, Northfield Publishing. 2009

NOTES

NOTES

NOTES

NOTES

15512768R00062

Made in the USA
San Bernardino, CA
27 September 2014